WALKS IN LIFE'S SACRED GARDEN

Ken & Pam,

May you lead poetic
lives that dance like the
sun, moon, and stars for
eternity.   love, Don

Poems by Donald Iannone

BOOKSURGE
An Amazon.com Company
Charleston, SC

WALKS IN LIFE'S SACRED GARDEN

ISBN 978-1-4196-6511-1

Cover Art: Adapted from Claude Monet's painting, *Monet's Garden, the Irises*, 1900.

Cover Design Assistance: Rend Graphics, Charleston, SC.

Dedication

To Mary.
Thank you for encouraging me to write my poetry. Most of all,
thank you for loving me. I love you very much.

Foreword

Walks in Life's Sacred Garden puts poetic words to life's irresistible music. The book's poems invite you to allow your feet and heart to sweep you away in the direction of the beauty, magic and mystery in your life.

The book's first chapter contains many spiritual and metaphysical poems. Some will make you ponder the very ground of your being, while others provide reassurance and inspiration that you can get to the other side of whatever challenge life has served up to you.

Mother Nature is the inspiration for the poems found in the second chapter. These poems will ignite your imagination about soaring hawks, fragile wildflowers, glorious fall leaves, desert sunsets, and much more.

The poems in the final chapter could be best described as *metaphysics in motion*, because they make you think, feel, laugh and cry about the everyday things we all experience in life. You will even find a few muses about poetry itself in the final chapter.

For me, poetry provides a wonderful excuse to stop, look, listen and touch life in a deeper way than I would otherwise. Hopefully *Walks in Life's Sacred Garden* will provide an excuse for you to do just the same.

Don Iannone
Mayfield Village, Ohio

Table of Contents

Chapter 1: Spiritual and Metaphysical Realities

Everyday life overflows with magic. The poems in this chapter provide tiny glimpses of this magic. Many are experiential in nature, growing out of meditation sessions, prayers, insightful dreams, peaceful and inspirational walks in the woods and deep conversations with family members and friends.

Life's magic awaits each of us. We are a part of this magic, and not separate from it. The challenge for most of us is to simply pay attention and experience the beauty and mystery of our magical spiritual birthright.

Across the ages, the world's spiritual and metaphysical traditions have worked to help us understand and experience the deepest and most mysterious parts of ourselves. While different words aim to describe this magic and mystery, common to all of these traditions is the belief that something much higher is present in our lives helping us find our way.

Hopefully these poems will help you touch the higher part of yourself, and carry you a few steps closer to the *light* inside you that can illuminate your path in finding your own deep life answers.

There are Deep Places

There are deep places
like valleys you wear
that you can't shake loose
until you give them
all that you have.

There are deep places
cutting your world in half
separating you
from your questions and answers.

There are deep places
sucking you in
and making you believe
there is a limit
to how far you can fall.

There are deep places
you must go
to find yourself
and lose the illusions
following you through life
like perpetual shadows.

There are deep places
that seem to surface
just about the time
you think you have life
all figured out.

Plumb these depths
but carefully
and never forget
these places are there
because your life starts and stops
and restarts again in these deep places.

Heaven: Come and Go as You Like

Heaven's doors are always open
  and all we have to do
  is walk in.

Too often
  we make the Holy too hard
  and too complicated.

Heaven's doors are open to all
  and receive all
  wishing to journey inward.

You can enter any time
  and leave any time.
Reservations are not required
  and no early withdrawal penalties apply.

You may be dying
  to go to Heaven
  but remember there is no need to die
  to get there.

The greatest thing about Heaven is
  there is nowhere you need to go
  and there is nothing special
  you must do to get there.

Working with Your Stuff

Working with your stuff
  in ways you haven't before.

Working with the stuff of your life
  to get it together
  heal
  and access the best part
  of who you are.

Working with your stuff
  to accept your stuff
  and be nothing more
  or less
  than you are
  and to live with yourself
  in perfect peace and harmony.

We Walk This Road But Once

We walk this road but once in life.

There is no stopping us once we're here—
until the road we travel ends, and then
a piece of us continues—
on another road
that we can't know—until
the road we're on has ended.

We come this way but once.
It is always the first time—
on whatever road we travel.
It is always the first time—
on whatever road we walk.

Next time we walk a road,
may we be gently reminded
we've walked other roads before.
But on this road,
we shall walk but once.

With the Feet God Has Given Us

God gave us feet
so we could take daily steps
moving us closer to Her.
She couldn't rightfully ask us
to follow Her, if
we didn't have a way
to get from where we are
to where She invites us to be.

Footloose at times,
we can be fancy free to wander
where our will entices us to go.
Our feet ground us, and
keep us sure-footed as the Capricorn,
steadfastly climbing Mount Everest.

Then at the top,
where our feet can take us no further,
we miraculously sprout wings, like Mercury,
lifting us into the sky, and
carrying us the rest of the way home.

Impermanent Being

There comes a time
　when we must go.
Before that time
　we don't know.
Seems unfair
　a secret to the very end.
But how much notice
　we cannot amend.
No matter how much time
　we have to be…
it's never enough for you or me.

Poetic Steps toward a Bleacher Seat in Heaven

Perhaps the best thing I do in life
is birth a single poem every day.
It seems the greatest defense
against life's bitter illusions,
trouncing last drops of honesty
flowing from my bedrock soul.

Perhaps the only thing qualifying me
for even a remote bleacher seat in Heaven
is the early morning verse tumbling
from my heart into my fingers, and finally
onto the blank page before my eyes.

Poetry alone can't save us,
but I'll take a bleacher seat
rather than no seat at all in Heaven.

When Silence Calls Us Home

The silence rings
throughout the room
I've lived in so long
and always called my home.

The silence shatters the mirror
in the room
I've lived in so long
and always called my home.

The silence cries lonely tears
that flood the well
outside the house
that for so long
I've called my home.

The silence speaks my name in words
only I can hear—
words calling me
forever home
to where the silence lingers still.

In this silence
I shall always rest
in my home
from now
till eternity.

Finding Your Conversation

Your life boils down to a conversation
that started at birth, and carries on
until the day it is over, or
until you decide you can carry it no further.

For most of us,
this conversation is like water:
trickling at times,
gushing at others, and
when it's really cold, freezing up
like a frozen pond in the midst
of a deep artic winter.

This conversation, flowing in all directions,
always finds its way back to what matters;
like why you suffer so
about your shortcomings,
or why you think
you are so unworthy of God's love.

Like all conversations, your conversation
must involve both talking and listening.
Always there must be another,
even if it's an imagined other,
for the conversation to take place.

Find your conversation—
the one in your deepest place.
Tune in to the words.

Listen first,
and once you've plugged in,
ask the hard questions:
those whose answers you fear the most.

Note: Inspired by a conversation and seminar with David Whyte, poet and author of *The Heart Aroused: Poetry and the Preservation of the Soul in Corporate America*.

Rise Above and Sail Away

Spread your wings
  like a bird, or angel
  and fly high above
  whatever cares or woes
  anchor you to your earthly suffering.

Fly away
  and soar
  like the eagle you are
  when God lights up your heart
  illuminating all those about you.

Rise above all illusions
  causing you to drift
  from reality's center.

Embrace the you encountered
  as all that you're not
  falls aside, and
  let's the real you sail away.

A Journey with No Beginning or End

Maybe like me
  you have hopelessly wondered
  at some point in your life
  how you will know
  when your spiritual journey has begun
  and when it is supposed to end.

If so
  these words by Zen master Dogen Zenji
  will resonate in your heart:
  "There is no beginning to practice
  nor end to enlightenment
  there is no beginning to enlightenment
  nor end to practice."

And so
  simply find joy in life
  as it comes to you
  and give up any notion
  that life is a race
  with any start or finish lines.

What is the Right Path?

There comes a time when
  each of us falls prey to wonder
  whether our path is the right path.

Rest assured that
  your path is your path.
Is it the right path?
Is it your path?
If it is your path
  then it is most assuredly the right path.

Some times
  it helps to remember that:
  "All paths are paths to God, because
  ultimately, there is no other place for the soul to go.
  Everything has come out of God
  and everything must go back to Him."

Look inside this path you follow
  and there you will find your God.

Note: Quote in italics by Paramahansa Yogananda, Indian yogi and guru, and author of *Autobiography of a Yogi.*

Cosmic Wisdom by the Fireplace

Be as you are
for being anything other
brings the death of you.

Be always as you can be
for being anything other
robs you of joy—
always your best friend.

Be true to your dreams
for they are your future
and they set the stage
for your infinite becoming.

Be open to the moment's lingering
for therein your soul resides.

Breathe in
and inhale truth's sweet fragrance.
For there
life's irresistible sweetness overtakes you.

Withholding Judgment on a Cold January Saturday Morning

A few arbitrary snowflakes tumble
   from the airy gray January sky
   like lazy marshmallows
   with no certain destination.

Just like life…tumbling down into
   and through us
   lacking any certainty beyond
   what the moment can know and teach us.

Einstein once said: *"Before God*
   we are all equally wise
   and equally foolish."

How foolish to judge the morning snow
   or its destination—
let alone life
   as it happens, and dances
   like a sure-footed ballerina
   spinning on the head of a pin.

The New You is Ready

Is your soul pushing you
   to turn in a new unknown direction:
   one having more light
   and one having more heart?

Is the old you getting in the way
   of the new you
   that is trying desperately
   to come into being?

Is your day filled with resistance
   causing you to wonder
   if you're possessed
   by some demonic force?

Do you find yourself...lost
   alone, afraid, and uncertain
   more than you find yourself at peace
   assured, happy, and connected to the universe?

Listen to your soul
   and its message
   that you are about to be reborn
   and the new you is ready to be.

Let the Morning's Silence Set You Free

Morning broke in silence
　only the heart can hear.
Her slow steady breath enraptured
　the dark sleeping trees
　whose silhouette forewarned
　a shadowless, but free, January day.

It has been said:
　"that we must always bear in mind
　that we are not going to be free,
　but we are free already. And
　that every idea that we are bound
　is only an illusion."
Let the morning's silence set you free
　as your shadow dissolves
　into the morning's next breath.

Note: Quote in italics by Swami Vivekananda, Indian spiritual teacher
and founder of the Ramakrishna Order of Monks.

Living

Live in hope,
For there, you can transcend,
Live in thanksgiving,
For there, you reap gratitude,
Live in wonder and surprise,
For there, you find joy,
Live in beauty,
For there, you find richness.
Live in truth
For there, your heart rejoices,
Live in balance,
For only there can you truly live.

Dancing with the Cobras inside Us

Silent desperate virtues float
like dancing flames on burned down candles
in the timeless cave of the heart.
Just a feeling you say. Maybe, but
isn't it funny how habits of character—
both good and bad,
seem to linger inside us,
and dance like magical king cobras,
spitting their venom into our lives.
Destruction and regeneration, both potentialities
inside us in any given moment.
Sometimes one, and other times another, but
all quiver inside us, like slowly burning candles
awaiting the right breeze to fan in our direction.

The Trouble with Life

The trouble with life
  is most of us live it
  fearing its inevitable end.

The trouble with death
  isn't dying, but
thinking we can escape it.

The trouble with time
  is the fiction it writes
  about eternity all over our lives.

The trouble with expectations
  is they drag you screaming
  from the moment, where
  the only peace exists, and
  where you always end up
  until the last moment
  passes through you.

Seeking Life and God Knows What Else

We circle life,
and life circles us.
All the while, it seems at times
we are so far away from life
and all else we seek.

On the surface, we know
the answers cannot be sought, and
that seeking is not the answer.
Deep down, however
an ancient program goes off,
and sets us on a chase
for something or someone
other than who or what we are.

It's easy to intellectualize, and say:
Why seek? There is nothing.
But then the search program—
more mighty than Google—
goes off and sends us chasing again
after our tails, and God knows what else.

All we can do is remind ourselves,
that we already have everything
we will ever need in life,
leaving us nothing to seek
and nothing to distract us
from enjoying what we already have.

Quiet Liberation

Caught up in the beauty
of a full moon December night.

Miracles part the clouds,
heavy with august snow—
falling hard, and
drifting slow motion across soundless yards.

No lunar madness,
or catastrophic emotional tidal waves
sweeping our hearts out to sea.
Only peace, and
an empty lingering sense of quiet liberation
rising in our soul's depths.

No urge to cry out,
like a moon-crazed wolf in the tall timbers.
Just undeniable primordial joy.

Caught, Captured and Let Go

Caught by will...
   somewhere between
     here and there
      and then and now.

Captured by grace...
   transcending all resistance
     letting go
      and letting God.

Abide in Your Own Emptiness

Exactly how big is the hole inside you
that you work day and night to fill?
All the things you throw into yourself,
hoping to fill the emptiness,
that grows deeper and wider
with every scoop of anything
you shovel into the hole.

It's strange how emptiness
attracts something...anything,
that promises to replace it
with anything other than emptiness.

Your emptiness is the real you—
the you that comes before all else,
including everything that fills you.
You are the vessel
that is filled with emptiness.

Embrace your emptiness.
Welcome it like a long lost friend.
It asks nothing of you,
nor does it ask you to be anything.
Be that empty vessel—
always open, and always receptive
to whatever the moment presents.
It is then that the true you can fill you.

Deep Soul Stirrings

Stirrings at the seat of the soul
  draw us into the deep waters.
To places beyond the light
  and all else we know.

In such places
  the light and what we know
  can be no guides
  because in these places
  the soul is the only guide.

We must walk as though
  we have heard our last call
  knowing that there is still life.

We must follow—
what seems an all too familiar voice
  as only the silence of the soul can speak.
We must slip beyond the words
  and into that place
where the soul must now carry us.

Living in the Moment

Never a day shall I weep,
Each precious moment I shall keep,
While weary I grow and so I sleep,
In my dreams life does seep.
I shall not tarry or fret too long,
For to the moment I do belong,
In so doing there is no wrong,
So there my life sings its song.
Our sight is bound to a glance,
If we're lucky there's a second chance,
To live it better and so enhance,
The life we live in joyful dance.
Look past yourself and you will see,
What's good in life and also free.
If you're willing to just let it be,
Each moment goes on for eternity.

The Beauty You Reflect

When you look
into the cosmic mirror,
what do you see?

Do you see
the astonishingly bright star
that I see
when I look at you?

Do you see
the deep pool
of crystal blue water
bathing the world in love?

Do you see
the elegant beauty of your own spirit
and the beauty you bring out
in others around you?

This is what I see
when I look at you.

My deepest wish is that
the mirror reflects the same
next time you venture a glance
into its surface.

Longing to Let Go

Some days your soul seems to wander,
in search of tattered memories and faded dreams.
Some days you long to retrieve your roots,
however twisted and convoluted they may be.
Some days you want your youth back,
the eager spring in your step,
and long days of just blissful play,
filled with honest imagination.
Some days you wish you could go back
and cut the painful ties holding you still
to things buried deep in the past.
Some days you long to be free
of all the addictions, compulsions, obsessions,
and even the dreams
that keep you from being truly free.
Some day you will care less
about all these things,
and surrender to the stars in the sky,
the carefree birds that sing in glee,
and the warm lapping waves
calling you gently to the beach.

In the Moment: Sunday 5:02 PM

Thin wind-swept clouds
  grace powder blue sky
    stretched overhead
      like a sheer linen canopy.

Mind in spacious expectation
  becomes pure sky
    absent all form
      resting formlessly
        rising from here to there
          only to fall again to here.

Expectation ceases.

Powder blue sky opens
  releasing self
    into foreverness.

Bearing Another's Cross

I saw him
  naked
  standing atop the hill.
He walked toward me
  bearing his cross.
I wasn't supposed to see his smile
  but I did.
As he disappeared over the hill
  his words glowed inside me:
Don't follow me
  for this cross is mine to bear.
Get down from your cross
  and carry your brother's
  that he may get down from his
  and carry another brother's cross.
And once all the crucified are free
  the light of all shall be joined.
And then, Heaven shall appear.

The Light That Holds Us

Be not afraid—
for your love
is strong enough
to lift you high above
the darkest night of your soul.

Lose not hope—
for there is a power
greater than even the sun
and whose light is so strong
we must close our eyes to see it.

Remember always the truth
that gave birth to you
and will always be with you
no matter how dark the night
or how cold the wind may blow.

A Tribute to All Who Have Suffered

Let the gentle being
that you are most deeply
fill the missing pieces
begging for the touch
of a loving hand.

May the many parts of you
grow together in harmony
like a beautiful tapestry
floating
in pure sunlight.

May each new breath you take
lull you high above the clouds
where peace lies waiting
to kiss away the tears
for so long you've cried.

And may magical harps play
familiar sweet lullabies
that weave threads of hope
into the soul
of the precious child within you.

When Sunlight Falters

Walking
  lost
  and alone
  in a long waking dream.
No way and no where to fly
  like the desperate half-melt snowflakes
  seconds before they end it all
  and turn back into water.
Lugging wherever we go empty canteens
  save one last drop of hope
  carrying us
  a few steps beyond
  to where the road ends
  and where new possibilities are born.
Sordid out of place fantasies dancing
  in the long dark shadows
  poking their way through the dying sun.
Pray to your god of self-understanding
  for fresh sunlight, for
  the old sun is dying.
Its rancid breath—
we can no longer stand.
Pray an end to the relentless pounding
  of heavy hearts, bearing witness
  to what must come
  and doesn't know its way.
Pray that the faltering sun
  doesn't lose its way for long.

What We Can While We Can

Sometimes the weight of life
is so heavy
you can't help but stumble
and sometimes even you fall.

Sometimes the speed of life
is so fast
you can't help falling behind
and sometimes
you never finish the race
seeming like yours to win all along.

Sometimes the twists and turns in life
set you spinning in circles
whose circumferences fail to intersect
even the tiniest part of your true nature.

Sometimes life goes on
without you
in directions you never imagined.
In directions not yours.
In directions, even at your best
you cannot go.

Sometimes the only thing
we have left
is the lingering glow
of life's fire burning on for those left after.

There Comes a Time

There comes a time
when sorting out
comes to an end
and the need to sort out
anything
becomes far less important
than nursing along
the time you have left.

There comes a time
when the end
no longer lingers
because
you have nothing left
to hold you back
and keep you from ending.

There comes a time
when all goodbyes have been said
and are over
and only the sound of silence
comforts and relieves
the pain of emptiness
weighing unbearably heavy
on your heart.

There comes a time
at last
when the need to end

ceases to be a struggle
and you finally accept
that life wasn't at all
what you thought it to be
rather it was
exactly what you allowed it to be.

Fresh New Possibilities by the River

It's been a long time
since I played by the river—
along the Mighty Ohio,
where I last knew myself
as an eager young boy.
Such unstoppable power
in the river, and in being young, and
in playing things real.

By the river, we played,
for hours on end.
Fishing, skipping flat rocks,
and dreaming—yes dreaming
of times not yet come, when
we'd be out of here,
and somewhere else
other than here.

Why is it so hard now to just play, and
dream of times not yet come?
Why is there so much pain
in gathering up fresh new possibilities
that carry you, like the river,
to another place you've not been?
Today, let me be that boy,
dreaming unstoppable dreams by the river.

Heart Fires Burn Brightly

A fire, well-stoked,
burns with tenacity and passion,
like a heart filled with love,
whose embers glow bright red and orange,
casting out the lonely darkness
that for so long cloaked its light.
Find your way—by the fire.
Rest there, as the night passes,
and as you engage the light,
enter finally into its midst.

Spread the Wings of Your Love

The sky is the limit
in terms of your love.
Reach high, and wide
in your quest to love the world
and everybody and everything in it.

Contrary to what you might think,
and at times even feel,
your love is endless, and abundant
beyond what your mind can grasp.
After all, love is a quality of heart,
and as such, is felt, not thought.

Spread your love,
like the wings of a glorious
full-blossom butterfly.
And while you're at it,
open to other's love.
It's there for the picking,
like fresh juicy strawberries
awaiting your sweet embrace.

The Second Hand

My wristwatch,
probably like yours,
has a second hand.
It goes around and around
the face of time,
cutting through nothingness,
creating and destroying the moments
with each clockwise tick.
I bill by the hour,
but live breath to breath,
like the second hand of my watch.

We worry too much about time.
It robs us of living...
downright cheats us out of life
that moves not only clockwise,
but in all directions simultaneously.
Your soul is timeless...
it knows nothing of your watch's second hand.

Listen!
Your soul is laughing at your obsession with time,
and what you miss between ticks
of your watch's second hand.

Awakening to Your Morning Dreams

Stand witness to the morning sun,
as she cuts through
the clutter of dreams
left behind by your spirit
on your still fluffy white pillow.

Embrace your new beginning,
as the clouds part,
allowing your heart to rejoice
in the newborn light of daybreak.

Resolve yourself to the reality
that how this day seems
flows directly from how you really are.

Appreciate early in this day
that the spirit-spun dreams
left behind on your pillow
may be your best shot at truth,
so long as you awaken to your dreams
before you sleep once again.

Until the Desert Night Once Again Falls

The desert night gasps for air,
like a seething tornado howls after
its own coveted perfectly still center.

Acetylene stars hang in pitch black sky
like crystalline Cinderella slippers
on a black velvet evening gown.

Too petrified to blink, our eyes lock
with the night's penetrating stare.

We long for the moon, but fear
the dreams it may birth in us,
crippling reality before its first awkward step.

The dunes cry mournful tears,
like those of a mother losing her only child.

I pray that one of the camels will move,
breaking the suffocating silence,
whose razor-sharp knife cuts deep
into the very jugular of our being.

Morning comes not a moment too soon,
and again we walk
until the desert night once again falls.

Avoiding Our Void with Fear

What is it that we fear
when we are afraid?
Look closely.
Observe your fear.
My fear is just more mind dust
trying to fill the unfillable void
emptying me into the endless river
beginning and ending nowhere.

Why do we work so hard
to fill the void inside us?
The void stands alone.
It is the only part of us that does.
All else requires something more...
something other that comes before and after.
The void needs nothing; not even you.
Once again, what is it you fear
when you are afraid?

Melancholy Stranger

He comes in the night—
that melancholy stranger,
whose footsteps you hear,
but only after he is upon you.
His night breath whispers
long silence in your ear.
You try not to listen,
but it's too late—
he has reached inside you,
and now possesses you as his own.
He comes and goes at will.
Haunting your peace,
stealing your joy, and
making you forget—
the sun rises every morning,
sweeping away the strangers from the darkness.

Plunge in Wonder

Wonder often,
Wonder wide,
Wonder further,
Never hide.
Never cease
to be amazed,
Delve deeper,
Delve wide.
Plunge the depths
for there to find
the truth you seek.
In stillness, there abide.

Sifting Sand

Life sifts
  like sand
  through open outstretched fingers.
No hourglass to contain it.
No beach providing a gestalt.

We play with it
  like some game
  we can win.

Don't bother tying up loose ends...
all ends are loose.
Just let it flow through you
  and wash you up on shore.
Celebrate wherever you are...
you're dead if you don't.

It fills us...
only to empty us
  spilling us on the floor
  abandoning our hope
  leaving us bare
  rubbed raw
  and finally...
just leaving us.

Darkness into Light

The night brews long,
The sun must wait,
Sing your song,
'cause it's your fate.

Listen for the three AM train,
And when it comes celebrate,
We all at times feel quite insane,
In places deep, love can't penetrate.

Lying there in the dark,
Wrapped in loneliness and despair,
Tonight you seem an easy mark,
For now, life seems so very unfair.

Questions hover like thick clouds,
Darker than the darkest night,
Rise above the somber crowds,
Don't give up without a fight.

Finally, when morning comes,
And the dark night has passed,
Your pain grows light and succumbs,
There your heart stands steadfast.

Greet the sun with a smile,
Let it fill you with soothing light,
Rest there in peace for awhile,
May your day be ever bright.

Living Moment by Moment

Your life is your life, but
it's also a piece of something much larger.
Your life is a gift, and
a priceless one at that, which
must be lived fully.
Your life is your creation, and
it's a direct outcome of all you think and do.
Your life is a mystery, even with
all the answers you think you have.
Your life is not a continuous,
cast-in-stone process, rather
it exists moment by moment.
Your life is not something separate
from who you are, instead
it is how your life looks
when you stare into the looking glass.
Your life neither stands before you, nor behind you;
those are illusions, causing you to forget
that your life is your life moment by moment.

Chapter 2: Nature's Call and Inspiration

The poems in this chapter were inspired by Mother Nature and her constant call that we come home to her. Our real home is within nature's arms. We are most at home when we are caressed by nature during a walk in the woods, a visit to a lovely flower garden, watching the birds and squirrels around the backyard feeders, listening to the ocean waves crash on the beach at night, or watching the sun bear its colorful soul on the western horizon as it sets.

Somewhere along the line, human beings got the idea that they are separate from nature, and can live outside nature's laws. Somewhere along the line, we got the idea that we are *"special."* Not only are these ideas untrue, but they are dangerous. We cannot know who we are in a spiritual sense until we come to terms with our inseparability from nature. If we are not careful, our belief that we are special grows into an inexcusable sense of entitlement that justifies us consuming nature's resources as though they existed only to satisfy our whims and desires.

Everything we ever needed to know in life is already written in nature's code. This code is accessible to anyone willing to look, listen, touch, smell, taste, and intuit everyday life's holdings. It's all there for us, even the poetry.

Sundown Geese

Four Canadian geese
  out of formation
    fly
      straight off
        into the setting sun.

No leaders
  just each following
    his own heart
      on this lingering
        March evening
          that wraps itself
            in the creamsicle orange sunset
            painting its way
              across the western sky.

One last glimpse
  of the fleeting foursome
    now just fading shadow shapes
      disappearing
        into sundown's last breath.

Visit from the Red-Tailed Hawk

From the window
we watched
not more than five yards away
the red-tailed hawk
perched regally
in the cold still crabapple.
Whitish belly prominent
and proudly fluffed
like a large down pillow.
Chocolate-brown plumage
painted across his head, nape and back.
Razor-sharp beak poised
and powerful talons grasping
the most hidden branch
out of view of unsuspecting songbirds
considering Sunday dinner
at the window feeder
by the dangling wind chimes.
Eyes like lasers
focused in all directions
missing nothing,
including the playful squirrel lost in himself,
and if not careful perhaps dinner
for our new raptor friend.
No songbirds appear
and so he lifts off
with broad wings pumping
the Airbus-like bird
high into the marbled gray March sky.

March

March winds howl without mercy.
Their wolf-like lungs ache—
inhaling bitter February air
not quite ready
to give over to April showers.
So we have March—
the in-between, go-between time
when kites either soar high
or fall abruptly
to the hard frozen ground below.
March winds cry—
into the night;
long past any hour of return.
Their voices drown out
winter's rebellious roar,
and spring's magical chant
that eventually coaxes early snow drops
to lift their frail heads
through still hard earth, and then
find the distant sun's white rays
that will grow strong enough
to still March's howl,
and steady spring's unpredictable dance
into the yellowing sun of summer.

Gifts

Moon swan on still water.
No ripples.
Only peace.

It's a gift...
the moon
  the swan
    the water
      the absence of ripples, and
the peace
  brought on
    by the stillness.

A Late February Arizona Sunset

A lone Harris hawk swoops and swoons
between shallow furrows cut
in the saguaro-carpeted mountains
just before Friday sunset.
Something about the tan bouldered rocks,
the endless azure sky, marbled
with slow drifting gray-white clouds,
and the slight glint of the near setting sun
on the hawk's out-stretched wings,
makes your heart long, and long deeply,
to be forever a part of this moment—
so close to turning orange and salmon-pink
before making room for the Arizona night sky.

Recovering through Reflection on a Snowy Saturday Morning

The fresh fallen snow brings welcomed silence
on a lingering gray Saturday morning.
It whispers and hushes,
as only a tender-loving mother can do.
It buries the agitation, frustration and stress
of a disastrous work week, turning
amusing dreams into horrifying nightmares.
The fresh fallen snow brings insulation
from the pain of self-doubt and self-flagellation—
both all to familiar ways in which
we abuse the beautiful spirits given us by God.
Once again, there is the reflection:
What really is the work we do?

Snow-Bound Tuesday

The winter cares nothing
about whether it is Tuesday,
let alone whether you're cold
and trapped under her heavy wet blankets.
She doesn't mourn your loss of time
due to impassable snow-clogged roads.
Frankly, she does only what she knows how to do,
which is to be winter,
complete with bitter blowing winds, mind-numbing cold,
and deep piles of silencing snow.
Don't blame winter for being true to her nature.
Heed her powerful message: be true to your nature.

Signs of an Early Spring

Sunset lingering brunt orange
in rock-like February clouds, hovering
in perfect blue sky, poised
to receive nothing less
than an early spring, quieted
by the lack of opposition
from a fast-moving winter, trundling
toward April, when once again
early wildflowers sing and dance their way
through winter's last remains.

Poetry on a Bitter Cold February Day

Bitter cold February wind
bites hard at my near numb cheeks
with its tiny razor-sharp teeth,
as I crunch my way down the driveway
to dig loose the now meaningless morning paper
from the crusty deep-drifted snow.
Fluffed up mourning doves huddle
and peck slow motion
for half-buried seed under the icicled feeder.
Angry winds gather and howl
through the skeleton-like tree limbs.
Lonely songs they sing
about broken unfulfilled dreams
dashed ever so long ago.
At twenty below, even the piercing bright sun
fails to permeate the artic air
that hovers thick like death.
For an instant, my mind warms
at the fleeting thought of spring
and fresh-born wildflowers.
But that too is snatched away
by the stinging wind,
that pours bitterness on any thought of relief.
Trudging back to the house,
I resolve to build an even larger fire,
and sit in quiet reflection,
until a poem comes to me.
Suddenly I feel one beginning to thaw.

Changes Spring Forth at Winter's Edge

We're almost there—
to spring that is.

While a heavy wet snow fell this morning
   winter knows by now
   that spring is inevitable, and
   little can it do
   to discourage spring
   from taking center stage.

Once the crocuses have had
   their chance to shine
   the daffodils will take the yard by storm.

And once the daffodils
   have gone daffy
   the orange, red, and yellow tulips
   will have their way—
   until the hungry deer discover them
   and mow them down.

So much change springs forth at winter's edge.

Observing January

Cold dark late January afternoon.
Snow clings, like fluffy lint
to frozen tree limbs shuddering
at the thought of three more months of winter.

Daylight fades, as afternoon gives way to evening,
and light wisps of snow now flurry their way
through openings pushed by winter's icy breath.

A lone sparrow in the distance
eyes the swaying feeder,
waiting for just the right moment
to descend for an early dinner
before darkness falls,
and the new moon rises.

Observing this Cleveland January day
my heart longs only to sit
by a blazing fireplace
and nurse a stiff scotch on the rocks.

December Daybreak

Deafening quiet December morning.
Still cold air surrounds and bites at nothingness.
Fresh white snow...piled deep, muffles
worldly worries and woes.
Light creeps slowly into the day, through naked trees,
awakening bright red cardinals,
plopping from perches into glittering snow
in search of first light breakfast.
No highway sounds, lawnmower roars...
only the sound of lingering stillness
hushing the heart into patient repose.

Encounters with a Long Winter's Night

I can't help but dream
on this long winter's night
when the fire blazes bright
and time stands perfectly still.

I can't help but drift
like the fresh fallen snow
that blankets the earth
and hushes me fast to sleep.

Somehow the purity and depth
of this early December snowfall
reminds me how simple life can be
when we just allow it to happen.

On this early winter's eve
the silence plumbs the depths
and awakens me while I sleep
stranding me amidst a single moonbeam.

Re-Embracing Tucson

To see once again the olive-brown Catalina Mountains
sweetly embrace the powder blue sky
and maze-colored Sonoran desert.

To behold a fire red sunset at Gates Pass,
making my heart soar as the sun sinks,
and spreading magical stardust on the Old Pueblo.

To smell the sweet pungent sage and Palo Verdes
after a short afternoon rain shower.

To feel the sacred earth under my feet;
walked so long ago by the ancient ones,
and even now feeling that same magical energy.

To return to Tucson one more time and re-embrace
what has long been a part of me.

Magic at the Water's Edge

It is the tide that gives birth to the grains of sand
  that become the beach
  that welcomes the tide's daily comings and goings.
And the tide is moved by light
  with the sun by day and the moon by night.
And so is life
  as each moment is born
  as the timeless tide washes over it
  giving the light what it needs to reflect upon.
And we find ourselves
  mere grains of sand on the beach of life
  created each moment by the magic.

Full Moon Buffalo Clouds

Odd buffalo-shaped clouds gallop
across the cold November sky.
I would have missed them completely
were it not for the perfect-circle full moon
glowing hauntingly bright at their backs.
Stripped of their leaves,
the naked skeleton-like trees reach into the sky,
as though searching for answers why
these near extinct clouds roam restlessly—
like my heart, which longs for peace
from its incessant wanderings.
Why does the light torment the darkness so,
and why does my heart suddenly long to be filled
by the moon and her secrets?

November

November arrives,
as lustful as bare wind on slackened sails,
Determined and forceful,
as only Scorpio can be, and always
secretive and magical in her poison sting,
The circles she spins...not beginnings of anything,
and not usually the end of anything, but
a time to be thankful for everything,
Also a time to celebrate pilgrimages, and
adventures to other worlds, that lie beyond
usual boundaries, and beyond
those normal parts of ourselves, that we wear
like costume jewelry to the theatre,
Her passionate skies wide open, and yield,
as only a woman can do,
ensnaring all she receives,
Her hypnotic smile intoxicates, and befalls
the unsuspecting seeker of her dark secrets,
November is here...I hear her spinning near.

Winter Night

By the golden fireplace we sat, listening
to the deep silence fall,
like the heavy snow, blanketing
the unflinching forest, lit with sharp edges
by the light of the near full December moon.
Stray fluffy flakes momentarily come to rest,
and then melt on the steamy windowpane.
The fire's flames rise and fall in lunar harmony,
casting faint shadows about the room.
We marvel that each moment seems so different,
much like the magical snowflakes.
On this night, the things mattering before,
now seem far less important,
as the silence of the winter night fills us.

First Snowfall

First snow fell
upon yards and woods
late last night
while we were sleeping.
Heavy flakes,
six-sided drops of baker's dough,
plopped here and there,
without warning or plan.
Tree limbs gasped and groaned
as mounds of slush
exploited their good nature.
The blustery winds—
we should have known—
an omen of first snow's coming.
But somehow,
the October leaves deceived us into thinking
we had more time.
Suddenly,
a child-like urge to play hooky
seized our hearts,
and we decided then
to sit by the window
and sip second cups of coffee.

Fallen Leaves

Battered tie-died leaves
tumble helplessly
to the waiting forest floor.
Unrelenting sheets of rain pummel
the trees' thick coats
into uncontested submission.
Naked and shivering,
the trees ready for winter's paintbrush
to color them in unadulterated whiteness.

October Full Moon

Why does the October full moon
seem so lonely, yet so bright?
Why does her luminous light
seem so still, without flicker?
Why does solitary moonlight
fill my dreams with deep mysteries,
keeping me awake as I sleep?
Why does the moon remind me
there is more to life
than what the sun can show?
Why do such questions stir and linger inside me
like hungry grey wolves
scouring the woods for prey?
Why is there no rest
until I make peace with the moon?

Snowy Forest Peace

I long for the snowy forest,
where the lone owl
speaks between snowflakes,
and where the wind takes my hand
leading me off into oblivion,
and where the quiet is so loud
I can't hear myself think,
and where the cold biting air
snaps reality like frozen tree limbs,
and where I find peace
waiting in silence under the giant hemlock,
and where God appears as sunlight
through snow-covered branches,
and where I stand awe struck
with tears streaming down my cheeks
for no reason other than my feeling alive.

Fall Magic

The glorious turning fall leaves
torture my sensibilities
with candy-sweet pleasure.
They leave me gasping,
like a diver submerged too long,
beholding the magical coral reef below.
They rip my heart out,
which goes chasing after whispering butterflies,
whose wings brush away lingering clouds.
And I thought early spring wildflowers
were hard to say goodbye to.

With Gentle Strokes She Paints

Fall hints
of her coming,
touching the leaves
with gentle strokes of color,
not unlike the painter
who starts out shy,
not knowing exactly where
her heart will carry the brush.
The masterpiece is complete, only when
her heart is full from giving.

Cleveland's Emerald Necklace

Emerald necklace--
green chain of forest being,
draped like Christmas garland
around Cleveland's shoulders.
Rich, deep, magical,
yet at times captivatingly introspective,
like a dark green Freudian slip,
worn loose and hanging below
the city's gray and blue silk dress.
As fall approaches,
and the air chills,
the jeweled necklace transforms
from just emeralds
to rubies, garnets, and golden sapphires.
And in winter,
the forest is aglow in diamonds,
sparkling bright as stars
on a clear winter night.
Every city has its gems—
Cleveland has its priceless emerald necklace.

When Catalina Eyes Touch You

Something deep inside me cries out
   as I gaze upon the sage-brown Catalina Mountains
   that stare back with soft reassuring eyes.
Eyes that say welcome home.
Eyes reminding me that Tucson
   will always be a part of me.
And every time I visit
   there will be a reunion.
A reconnection with something deeply loved
   and deeply felt
   like a star-filled Arizona night sky.
And every time I breathe in a Tucson sunset
   something will always be revived
   and relived like a an ancient mythical journey
   through time and back home again.
Something magical always happens
   when Catalina eyes touch you.

The Crickets' Autumn Song

Solitary crickets drone on
through the night's deepest hours
about fall's impending ascent.
They tell poignant epic stories,
which they never quite finish,
leaving last lines for the winter sun
to write on fresh-fallen snow.
The crickets' hypnotic chirping drowns out
the 12:07 am train, almost passing unnoticed,
except for the squealing rails, stretching
from one end of the night to the other.
Summer died suddenly, but gloriously,
like the fuzzy green caterpillar, who morphed
in one afternoon into a graceful butterfly.
The crickets just do what they do,
without being asked, or being rewarded.
For they sing in a voice heard by the turning leaves,
the fading grass, and swelling pumpkins,
who otherwise might miss their time.
When I was young, I was too busy
to hear the crickets sing.
But now autumn rises up in me,
and I ready for the winter sun
to once again write last lines
in the fresh-fallen snow.

along a deep forest trail

penetrating
deep green
woodland forest
hemlocks and oaks tower
high above.
pine needle floor rises up
like an excited green phoenix
wild
beyond control
without reason
unrelenting
in his campaign to be free of all
even the golden-yellow sun
that trickles
through near impenetrable green.
there a new beginning erupts
like a galaxy of stars
naked
without expectation
only a heart to guide
its unfolding.
there upon the forest floor
a single seed falls
and life once again begins.

Near Night Moment

The sunset bleeds a delicate rainbow
of oranges, yellows, scarlets and reds
across the fading blue summer Arizona sky.
Just barely within ear shot,
the first coyote yelps in approval
of the melting pastel masterpiece.
His voice, like the moment holding it,
follows the wind and the sun into the west,
where all are swallowed by the hungry night.
Dark edges form along the tree tops,
haunting them with secrets
that the night will hide until morning.
A slight breeze gathers out of nowhere,
carrying the scent of wild sage and sweet acacia,
stinging our noses with pleasure.
Daybreak will bring an even more spectacular sunrise,
but our wedded hearts long
to hold this near-night moment.

One Hot July Morning

White-hot July sun drops beat
like a heavy rain of fire bricks
on the flower garden
nestled along the white picket fence.
Normally spry orange day lilies and pink wild roses
droop for cover
as Monsieur Soleil tightens his grip
on all in his path.
The Huck Finn-looking young lad next door
sits bent over, like a limp rag, in the steamy grass
picking his dirty toes in silence.
Even the red-throated hummingbird's wings
are quiet and motionless
sensing the danger of spontaneous combustion
with the slightest movement.
Waves of oppressively hot air
waft into the open kitchen window
crushing my usual desire for morning coffee
or anything short of a freezing-cold lime popsicle.
I think only of standing naked
for hours in a freezing cold shower.

Sedona Rainbow

Dedicated to Mary

The rain will fall so love it all
In the distance, wild birds call,
You, like a magical rainbow, appear
Bringing undying hope and good cheer,
Days and night blur happy as larks
Soaring high leave their marks,
High school melodies sweet to the touch
Never one I've loved so much,
Eagerly awaiting each precious moment we share
Nothing much else do we care,
Sixteen years together we've been
Never a better time, I can't think when,
Ahead we think, but today we live
More and more we have to give,
On this 24th day of June you shall always be
A Sedona rainbow just for me.

An Arizona Rainbow

Milky gray clouds give way
to blurred streaking pastel colors,
arched in celebration
across the darkened Arizona sky.
Hard lines dissolve
in the sky and in my heart
into misty half circles,
dipping down deeply
like magical paintbrushes,
dripping luminous watercolors
across the early evening sky.

Tucson Brush Strokes

Nothing hides the searing hot sun
at noon in June in Tucson,
where the maize-colored desert sand
befriends the olive-green sagebrush,
and the gangly octopus-armed saguaro
stretch lazily in a perfectly blue sky,
and where ragged dull gray-green mountains
cradle you in their powerful arms,
while the old pueblo sleeping inside you
slowly melts back into its original abode.

More Precious than a Rainbow

Some where in time
lies a magnificent rainbow
with your name on it.
Somewhere outside time
lies an inner emptiness, far more
precious and lovely than your rainbow.
Nowhere and at no time
has the reality of your own being
been more clear and powerful
than in this very moment.
Reach out gently,
and touch its wing, without grasping—
at yourself or the moment.

Late Summer Visions

Late summer zinnias wait
more patiently than mountains
for last drops of sunlight,
keeping them in color.
The door to the old barn,
just beyond the desperate flowers,
has decided it will never close.
At its age,
there is nothing left to hide.

Chapter 3: Living on the Everyday Human Plane

Until we have learned the important lessons that life has to teach us, we are stuck here on the human plane writing poetry, or doing whatever it is that you do with your life. Not quite the realm of the mythical gods and goddesses, but our humanity allows us to learn, and that is what is most important to the creation of a happy and successful life.

Life has its moments of joy and sadness, and over time, we come to see both as teachers about just how precious life is. As I mentioned earlier, poetry is an excuse for me to experience life more fully on an everyday basis than I might otherwise do.

The poems in this final chapter speak to our strength and frailty as human beings. Some might make you laugh, and some might make you cry. Each, in its own way, urges you to walk deeply into life's sacred garden and discover the special gifts that await you there.

Is Your Work Worth It?

Work is not all it is cracked up to be.

It's filled with pain and suffering
killing off people's joy and sense of meaning,
and it is killing off people—
causing them to die of work-related stress and strain.
*"For what shall it profit a man, if he shall gain the whole world,
and lose his own soul?"*
A Biblical thought worth embracing.

We've missed the mark...badly,
when it comes to the role of work in life.
If your heart is so heavy
that you can't rejoice at the sunrise,
and your mind is lethally poisoned
at the thought of the work you do,
then it is time—
time to let go of your work,
and the pain you attach to it,
and the pain it attaches to you.
Be careful what you say yes to today.
If your work doesn't please your spirit,
say no to the work you do.

Your work will not get you into Heaven,
whatever you think Heaven might be.
Don't allow yourself to be used by others
in the name of work, a job or career.
Don't enslave yourself to your work desires.

There is no end to the work treadmill, which
like all treadmills, goes nowhere.

Look carefully at who is ultimately served
by whatever work you do.
Is it the stockholders of the company,
who care nothing about you,
except whether they make $100,000
for every dollar you earn?
Is it the ego-maniac shift supervisor,
who was abused as a child, and
believes he is entitled to strip you
of your dignity and sense of well-being?
Who is served by your work?
Maybe it's your own maniacal ego
that persists in clinging to its illusions
that your work is you.

Honor yourself today
by seeing your energy and attention
as supremely sacred.
Be cautious where and how
you invest that energy in your work.
Put an end to your own slavery.
Only you can set yourself free.

Freeman

The checkout line was short—
Just me and one other man,
who I was certain had something to tell me,
and so I said good morning
to this tall, weathered-faced older Black man
with large ham-sized hands.

He introduced himself as Freeman,
and asked me if I knew why.
Before I could answer,
he interjected *"because I am a free man!"*
At loss for words, I smiled
and managed a half cheerful *"I'm glad to hear that."*

*"Forty seven years I spent in the big house,
and now I'm free."* Freeman added.
"That's a very long time" I replied.
Freeman jumped back in *"That's no lie.
I was only eighteen when they locked me away.
Wanna know why?"*

Of course I wanted to know why,
but I didn't want to seem too eager to find out.
Freeman went on *"Killed a man once
because of what he did to my sister.
He deserved it, and I confessed.
There was no denying it.
Even the judge said the man deserved it.
Trouble is...you can't go around killin' folks*

just because they done something wrong.
I'm not proud for what I done, but
I paid my price—forty seven years in hell;
a place you never want to go.
But today, I'm standing in line a free man,
buying a newspaper,
with another free man I don't even know,
but I'm so happy I could cry."

I extended my right hand to Freeman, which
he grasped with a calloused sweetness
I will never forget.
I saw the tears amidst his grin.
As I drove away, I did the math.
Freeman was locked away in 1960.
I was nine, and
we had black and white television back then.
I think the world back then
was pretty much the same
as the TV set we watched most evenings.

Martini at a Country Bar

Strange town, strange bar.
Long day, long face.
Filled room, no seats, I'm shot.
Vodka martini in hand, relief in sight.
Country music, not my style...
but this is rural Pennsylvania,
and I'm a city slicker from Cleveland.
Nasty smell...burned popcorn.
Fat man, cigar, saddle shoes.
Retake...saddle shoes, fat man?
No way...not in a country bar
out here in the sticks!
Nasty smell, not popcorn...who knows what.
Chug-a-lug, martini glass empty.
Cheeks warm, head numb.
Even this dingy place begins to look better.
Bar maid with big teased red hair pushes drinks
across the bar to eager customers,
working on leaving reality.
The idea for this poem pops into my head.
That's it!
Time to blow this joint...
no cotillion likely here tonight.

In Search of a Metaphysical Explanation Why Two Toilets Crap Out at the Same Time

Crappers crap out—
even the best of them, and
that would be a Toto, or
so says our $150 an hour plumber.
Did you know toilets breakdown
for a lack of use, as well as over-use?
Go figure.

I wouldn't be kidding if I said
all this beats the crap out of me.
Why would two fine, upstanding commodes
bite the dust at the same time?
Reincarnation plans together?

It would be different
if we had young hooligans about the house,
who thought flushing tennis balls
was an entertaining way to spend
a cold, snowy Sunday afternoon.

Well, the good news is
we are the proud parents of
two identical twin Toto toilets.
Both just waiting
to show us what they can do.
Can't wait to give them a test drive.

The Golden Pig Baby Business

No reduction this year
in China's population.
Crossover the pig and gold
in Chinese astrology,
and you get millions
of lucky new Golden Pig babies.
Notice I didn't say *baby pigs*!
Happens every sixty years—
that's five years short
of the years needed for you and me to retire.
We should be so lucky,
or be a Golden Pig baby.
Auspicious or suspicious?
Maybe some of each.
Does it matter?
Not really.
Mother Nature will ultimately weigh in
on China's popping Golden Pig baby population.
Don't mean to sound cynical, but
ask Proctor and Gamble, Toyota,
or any other major corporation across the world
porking up on the fertile Chinese market.
For them,
it's the Year of the Golden Ringing Cash Register.
So, bring on those Golden Pig babies.

Feline Tornado at 1:56 AM

Nothing rests or finds comfort in the house,
when the three tan-brown and white calicos
run amok in the late night shelter
of a fresh-blown full moon.
Nocturnal by nature,
the full moon rushes through their feline veins
like XXX strength java coffee.
Blame their mania on global warming,
or an electromagnetic overload
from too many electrical devices in the house,
but deep down you know—it's their nature.
Look at their crazed eyes glowing in the dark,
like runway landing lights at the airport.
For God sake don't move...
your shins will be bruised below recognition,
like battered prize-fighters going into the last round.
Like tornadoes,
ripping their way across flat-ass Kansas,
the calico trio's night high must run its course.
God help us all
if the full moon lingers one more night.

Mind and Form: A Poem on Esoteric Thought

It burrows its way through life like a mole.
Seeking and creating as it seeks,
and whatever it creates, it seeks again,
because it now knows its target.
Yes, the mind forever leaves its traces--thoughts,
some idle and lame, some subtle and deep,
some indiscernible from feelings and bodily movements.
Not just some organ in your head,
like your boozed out liver,
or your burned out lungs.
It's more like the air you breathe—
it's everywhere inside and outside you.
Mostly you think it's inside you,
but it's also outside the embodied you.
It's a creature and creator of habit.
It adores form, and
simultaneously abhors and delights
at the formless and unmet in life.
It loves form because each form
is a familiar and known furrow
created by an earlier burrow.
It loves the formless and unmet too,
because each is a conquest
to sculpt a form from the formless.
Over time, the mind learns to love itself,
and so it clings to itself and its creations, because
these are its children—
its offspring offered to all it has created, and
the make-believe separate external world,

which it has also created as a plaything, and
as a form against which to forge other forms.
It can only think of itself as a form
because it has low self-insight,
and only sees that which it has formed.
Its true nature, I believe, is formless, and yet
the mind can only grasp the formless as a form.
How sad, you say, that your mind
cannot grasp its true nature.
Don't sadden yourself with such machinations.
Even your sadness is a form, created by your mind,
as a futile attempt to give form to itself.
The answer? Don't go there either...
for answers are also illusory forms
seeking formless questions...
that are nothing more than your mind's gropings
to transcend form and reach formless permanence.
Next time you decide to visit reality, whatever that is,
don't think about it.

*Warning: Don't take any of this seriously. It could lead to life
threatening illusions.*

When the Security Alarm Calls Your Name

Wednesday, 4:16 AM.

Security alarm screeches out in the night.

Hearts jump out of our chests.

Cats streak out of the bedroom.

Confusion and terror all at once.

Groping for the light.

Fumbling to turn off the alarm,

but not too quickly in case...

there is a real threat.

Alarm panel flashes "PHONE."

Phone? What the hell?

Oh, the phone must not be working,

and the security system ties into the phone line.

Check the phone.

Checking...

Dead as a door nail.

Call security company...on the cell phone, because

the regular phone line is...dead.

Security people conclude the obvious:

Sir, your phone line isn't working.

Duh!

Don't you love experts?

Ok Ma'm, so how do we shut off this blaring alarm?

Sir, power down the system.

What? How do I do that?

Go to the basement, and

I will instruct you on the procedure.

Procedure?

Ma'm, I know nothing of these things.
I think, but don't say:
Fixing things skips generations in my family.
And guess what? It skipped me.
Alarm still blaring...
obviously the neighbors hate our guts
for our alarm awakening them two hours early.
Standing in my bathrobe,
with my Albert Einstein morning hair,
I succeed in powering down the alarm system.
Finally it's silent.
The cats are nowhere to be found for two hours.
I look everywhere.
How do they know how to hide so well?
Must be genetic, like my lack of mechanical aptitude.
An unexpected spiritual moment overtakes me...
Live in the moment...that's what your alarm in telling you.
I think...shit. I just want my coffee.

Rainy Night in Kokomo

From my stale-smelling hotel room window,
I watch the warm August rain pound Kokomo,
like a unbeaten prizefighter
pummeling the neighborhood sissy.
I hate the rain,
sometimes even more than raw oysters—
slippery disgusting bastards that they are.
Almost 9 PM and still light.
No moon or stars tonight.
Just heavy clouds pissing on K-Mart shoppers
madly dashing to their beater cars.
Have you ever really studied the carpet in a hotel room?
Not exactly the Marrakech Express.
All those grimy toe jams—
the sort you wiped on your younger sister
and made her cry when you were kids.
This place is pretty clean,
compared to some places I've spent the night.
I remember discovering dust balls
the size of African Bush elephants
under my bed in a flea bag hotel in Erie
not too long ago.
There's no privacy in a place like this.
The poor SOB next door
should either lay off the bean dip
or save his cherry bombs for July 4th.
No need for a wake-up call in this joint.

Fly for Supper

Tiny spider,
Tiny spider,
How stealthfully you crawl,
Across the floor and on up the wall,
You spin a quick web to snare your prey,
I'd guess you do this six times a day,
You sit so still, the whole time you stare,
Awaiting the big-eyed fly perched on the chair,
Somehow you know just when he will fly,
And land on the wall oh so high,
The fly flaps his wings starting his flight,
You imagine his landing perfectly right,
Off guard you catch him, he lands in your web,
And he is your supper just like I said.

Artful Living

Life is creative.
We have choices
between the moments
that paint our life canvas.
Leading an artful life
gives life its meaning.
What is art?
It's what we are.
Never perfect,
but always imperfectly what we are.
Art is what we make of our lives.
For me...poetry is one dimension.
Relationships another.
Work still another.
Even money is art.
Remove the change from your pocket.
Look at it closely.
We make it, so money is also art.
Today is a work of art
we are in the process of creating.
Tomorrow, just a gleam in our eyes,
leaps from the creative depths within us.
Live artfully.
But remember…
you have to live with whatever you create.

Why Do I Drive Myself So Hard?

No matter how I try
I can't shake loose the hold
of the interstate accident
I witnessed last month.

The images of the dead bodies
seem to hover in my mind.
I saw them—
the dead bodies,
completely covered by sheets.

People alive in one instant
and dead in the next.
People on their way to somewhere
when something went terribly wrong
and now their lives have suddenly ended.

Two people
who won't go home tonight
to their families,
eat supper,
and complain about their jobs.

Two people
who never intended to die this way,
or for that matter in any way
on this snowy cold early February morning.

I wonder who was at fault—

if anyone at all was to blame
for what had happened.
What good is blame
at a time like this any way?

The two people on the covered gurneys
are just bodies now, waiting
to be loaded into the ambulances
with the flashing red and blue lights, and
then taken through the snowy darkness
to a nearby small town hospital,
where those who love them
must come at this early hour,
identify their bodies, and
somehow accept
they will never see their loved one again.

The bodies have names—
even now at this dark hour,
as their spirits slip away,
and their loved ones hover over them,
saying their names, hoping
the names will bring them back to life.

Why was I driving so fast this morning?
Why was I not paying attention to the traffic,
the slippery road, and
my hurried, over-stressed, out-of-control life?
I could have caused this accident
by leading my life in such a reckless fashion.

I could be one of those lifeless bodies,
covered by a stark white sheet, waiting
to be taken to a hospital I don't know,
and my family would have to come
and identify my remains.

Why do I drive myself so hard in life?

Cleveland's Lake Erie

Proud, but smaller than her four siblings,
Erie wraps herself,
like a rough hewn blue-gray shawl
around Cleveland's burly brown and green shoulders.
She hugs the city in places,
giving needed comfort and reassurance.
Then, like any beautiful woman,
she steps back and flirts at a distance—
even sometimes defying our advances.
Her shallow waters seethe at times,
standing tall and swaying back and forth
like a quiver of king cobras.
Her current four thousand year-old incarnation
remains hard to fathom, let alone
her Pre-Pleistocene Ice Age roots,
stretching back over two million years.
With age comes grace, and surely
this fair lady commands our respect
for her deep flowing wisdom and beauty.
All this said,
why is such scarce notice given by us
to this watery Cinderella to our north?

When a Factory's Life Ends

The foul gray smoke that once belched
from the tall red brick stacks
was a bittersweet sign of life—
that the old factory was still working.
The smoke has now ended,
along with the noisy metal-banging,
that for so many years kept men busy
from sun up till sun down.
The iron gates are chained shut,
and never again will greet the dark faces of the hardened men
with stale breath from strong black coffee and cigarettes.
It's too easy to blame too many strikes
for the factory's foreboding silence,
but hungry workers elsewhere,
willing to work for much less,
and customers needing less metal,
are just as much the reason
why the dark faces have grown much darker.
The mill is history—
a cold, lifeless archeological ruin,
and so are the paychecks that paid the bills
and gave some small consolation to the two thousand men,
who laughed at each other's lame jokes,
and dreamed of days when they wouldn't have to work so hard.
Now that day has come,
and their dreams and jokes have ended,
but they're not laughing.

All's Not Well in the City

Abandoned hopes grow
like incurable cancers
in brownfields in the city.
Lifeless forms walk
downtown's empty streets
in search of make-believe shadows.
The clock on the square
is not only broken
but lost in time.
Factories once filled
with buzzing machines and workers
are graveyards where dog-sized rats
feed on rusted metal and scum.
Early every morning
even before you wash your face
the local newspaper pours raw acid
into the eyes of suffering citizens
who flip hamburgers for a living
and who worry late into the night
about how to live in a dying city.
Service is a thing of the past
in the remaining stores where you shop.
Nobody even cares enough to hope in a town
where good sports teams are moored to self-defeat
even before the season begins.
Political elections are nothing more
than depraved freak shows
featuring vampires and demons
sucking the last drops of life out of the city.

Everyone denies
in their own way
that we have a real problem.
It's a black spot on the city's soul
that is growing larger everyday
and only a massive exorcism can remove it.
So don't bother acting surprised
that nobody wants to live here.
That is just your way
of denying we have a real problem.

A January Encounter with St. Louis

Beloved river city,
nestled on the west bank
of the mighty Mississippi,
that magically snakes through you,
and connects you to other river cities.
Your roots grow deeper by the day,
while your future arches its back
like an awakening calico,
warming herself in the afternoon sun.
You've seen many dark nights,
when the moon fails to glow,
yet starlight continues to grace your soul.
Lazy snowflakes flirt with the biting westward wind...
a wind you know so well
on this late January afternoon.
You toy with me in word and image,
daring me to grasp you about the waist
and dance on tiptoes with you
into the westward-leaning sun.
South of you at Cairo,
the industrious Ohio joins your Mississippi.
At your right elbow, ancient Cahokia's 20,000 souls
have restlessly slept now for more than 600 years.
Farther south, midway to Memphis,
nobody wants to talk about New Madrid,
where the earth shakes off excess energy
on a regular basis, and where in 1811
the Mississippi reversed her flow...

a feat not since accomplished,
nor even wished.
You are a city of poets and writers,
entrepreneurs, athletes, actors and scientists.
A city prone to division at times,
but once again learning to come together
around what means most in life.
You are a city mattering to so many,
even those begrudging the redbird his special feast
on tiger last October.
My simple wish for you, Oh St. Louis,
is happiness sparing none,
and may you, in your unfolding urbane glory,
never cease to amaze.

The Christmas Tree Outside Our Front Window in Martins Ferry

Growing up in Martins Ferry in the 1950s,
there was a magical Christmas tree
just outside our front window.
Adorned with fresh driven snow,
and every bit as lovely as the tree
gracing our living room,
with its bright ornaments,
shiny lights, and sparkling tinsel.
The beautiful evergreen in the front yard,
seemed to reach forever upward,
bending whenever necessary,
but always springing back.
During the day, the sunlight made its ice crystals glitter,
like the stars that shone so brightly
above it in the dark winter night sky.
The birds knew of the tree's specialness,
as they flocked to its branches,
like bees to honey.
I loved the mighty evergreen
for its fortitude in withstanding
the winter's brutal assaults,
and I loved its vibrancy—always green,
and always willing to give of itself
to all needing food and a place to rest.
Were it not for this wonderful tree,
I might know nothing
of the true meaning of Christmas.

Rainbows on Dusty Country Roads

When we were young
we walked ordinary country roads
in search of hopes and dreams.
The road itself didn't matter, really.
Back then, the road didn't even need color,
for we were rainbows ourselves,
following something larger,
something more significant,
than the country roads we walked.

We tolerated the boney dust,
stirred by a lone '57 Ford pickup truck.
Even the hot noonday sun
beating down on our heads
didn't take our minds away
from the river of dreams
that swept us inside,
and away from the world,
where boys walked country roads,
leading nowhere, and yet anywhere
their dreams could take them.

We would do it over again…
that is walk dusty country roads,
if we could be young again,
and if we could be desperately possessed
by dreams that stirred our souls,
and made us feel alive.
After all, what else is there?

Hyacinths Growing by the Old Gray Fence

Why ever do the hyacinths grow
next to the dying gray fence
on the east end of the farm?
Nobody ever goes back there.
Who's going to ever see them?
Beauty like that shouldn't be wasted
where there is no eye to see.
They're stubborn—
downright hard-headed,
hiding there next to the old fence.

I came back a couple weeks later,
and they were gone.
Just like the beautiful sunset from last night.
Just like my grandmother
who lived on the farm
when the fence was brand new.
Why ever do those hyacinths grow
next to the dying gray fence
on the east end of the farm?

The Poet's Pain

I wonder seriously
if I'd have my poetry
if I didn't have my pain.
You may smile smugly, thinking perhaps
you know my pain.
Rest assured, you don't, and
frankly, there's no need for you
to know my pain.
After all, it's mine, and
you have your own pain—
giving rise to your poetry, maddening dreams,
insufferable prognostications, fits of sexual hallucination,
or even drunken spells leaving you numb.
Yes, poets suffer...
not first with their poetry, but with life.
And those reading poetry suffer too...
not with the poetry they read, but also with life.
I think of Oscar Wilde, who once said:
"We are all in the gutter,
but some of us are looking at the stars."
Wilde's point isn't that misery loves company, rather
some of us are more able to use our misery
to see life whole, including its pain.
For some of us, poetry is our weapon of choice
in seeing the reality of pain,
without the rose-colored glasses.

Just a Poem In Between

What do you do when
someone gets inside you—
someone you never knew you knew
and suddenly
they are a deep part of you?

What do you do
when something you've dreamed of
when you were both asleep and awake
magically appears
from the other side of the mirror?

What do you do
when your fading reality
creates choices you don't want to make,
setting you adrift in the tide
washing you hopelessly out to sea?

What do you do
when a kindred spirit overtakes you
like a serene tsunami
and you are left drowning
in your own feelings
you never knew you had?

What do you do
when something beneath
your conscious mind

spills you into another galaxy
you are speechless to describe?

You write a feeble poem
hoping it will save you from yourself
and from what you might do
if there wasn't at least a poem
between you and this new reality.

The Word Charmer

Cobra-like words
dancing on empty unlined pages,
Following their creator's hand
side to side and up and down,
Merging briefly with the hand
that feeds them,
Tempted at times to bite it,
then quickly dancing away,
At times, mouthing the words
with slippery pointed tongue
and thick red lips—so large
even the dictionary could hide behind them,
Releasing them finally like soft bubbles
drifting in thin air,
Charming hard women into ladies
and calloused men into well-mannered young boys,
Words snaking their way inside you,
making you squirm and shudder
as they fill your heart,
As they bring back the dead part of you,
buried long ago but never forgotten,
Beware the word charmer—
he becomes you and you become him.

A Poem to Get Up My Batting Average

If you write one poem a day for a year
  you have enough for a book of poetry.
Of course, not all poems make it into the book
  since many say the same thing just in a different way
  and some poems, no matter how hard they try
  say nothing to the poet or the reader.
And so why include them?

Over the past twelve months
  this poet wrote 361 poems.
Only 114 were deemed good enough
  by this poet to make the book.
If you're a baseball player
  that means you had a .316 batting average for the season.
Not bad all things considered.
Ok, it doesn't come up to Ty Cobb's .366 lifetime average
  but it's close to Roberto Clemente's .317 lifetime average
  who happens to be my all-time favorite baseball player.

Hoping to match Roberto's average
  I gave myself one more at bat.
It's a line drive down the left field line.
Was it fair or foul?
I'll let you be the judge.
In any case, this is the last poem in this book.

About the Author

Don Iannone is a poet, writer and consultant living and working in Mayfield Village, a suburb of Cleveland, Ohio. He runs a small strategic planning and organization development consulting company that helps communities increase their economic prosperity. He has worked across the United States and selectively in other countries.

Walks in Life's Sacred Garden is Don's second published collection of poetry. His first book, *Stilling the Waters*, was published in 2005. Several of his poems have also been published in various online poetry journals.

His online poetry journal, *Conscious Living Poetry Journal*, contains many of his poems. Please stop by and visit Don at: http://conscious-living.blogspot.com.

660014

Made in the USA